PIANO • VOCAL • GUITAR

Best of the Jackson 5

Photograph by Fin Costello / Redferns

ISBN 1-4234-0357-6

HAL•LEONARD®
CORPORATION
7777 W. BLUEMOUND RD. P.O. BOX 13819 MILWAUKEE, WI 53213

In Australia Contact:
Hal Leonard Australia Pty. Ltd.
4 Lentara Court
Cheltenham, Victoria, 3192 Australia
Email: ausadmin@halleonard.com

Visit Hal Leonard Online at
www.halleonard.com

8   *ABC*

3   *Dancing Machine*

23   *Get It Together*

12   *I Am Love (Part 1)*

16   *I Am Love (Part 2)*

30   *I Want You Back*

34   *I'll Be There*

46   *Lookin' Through the Windows*

39   *The Love You Save*

50   *Mama's Pearl*

62   *Maybe Tomorrow*

59   *Never Can Say Goodbye*

66   *Sugar Daddy*

DANCING MACHINE

Words and Music by WELDON DEAN PARKS,
HAL DAVIS and DONALD E. FLETCHER

At the drop of a coin she comes a - live, yeah! _ She knows _ what she's do - in';

she's su - per bad now, she's geared to real - ly blow your mind.

1

2

ABC

Words and Music by ALPHONSO MIZELL,
FREDERICK PERREN, DEKE RICHARDS and BERRY GORDY

With drive

Buh, buh, buh, buh, buh, boo, buh, buh, buh, buh, buh, buh. You

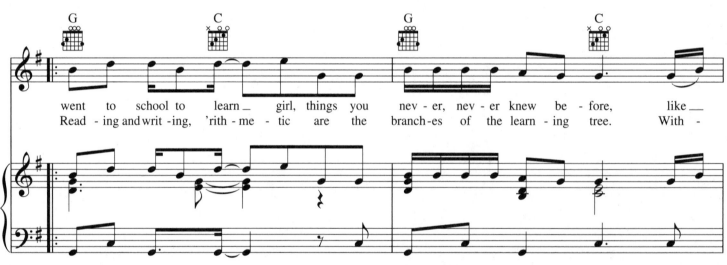

went to school to learn _ girl, things you nev-er, nev-er knew be-fore, like _
Read-ing and writ-ing, 'rith-me-tic are the branch-es of the learn-ing tree. With-

"I" be-fore "E" ex-cept af-ter "C" and why two plus two makes four. Now, now, now _
out the roots of a love ev-'ry day, girl, your ed-u-ca-tion ain't com-plete.

Bass Vamp

I AM LOVE
(Part 1)

Words and Music by MEL LARSON, JERRY MARCELLINO,
DON FENCETON and RODERICK RANCIFER

Relaxed and soulful

watch you
won - der

as you go ____ from day to day.
of why ____ I've been mis - used.

The eyes of love will
I find my - self in

Come back, lov - er, come back, this is where you be - long. _____

Come back, lov - er, come back, this is where you be - long. _____

where you be - long. _____

Segue to Part 2

I AM LOVE
(Part 2)

Words and Music by MEL LARSON,
JERRY MARCELLINO and DON FENCETON

Fast Progressive Rock

Segue from Part 1

Guitar solo

continue Guitar solo

GET IT TOGETHER

Words and Music by BERRY GORDY,
HAL DAVIS, DONALD E. FLETCHER,
JERRY MARCELLINO and MEL LARSON

Bright Funk

You bet- ter get it to - geth - er, or leave it a - lone.

If you don't want my lov - in', I'll be gone.

Get up, get up, get up.

*Recorded a half step higher.
**Male vocal is sung at written octave.

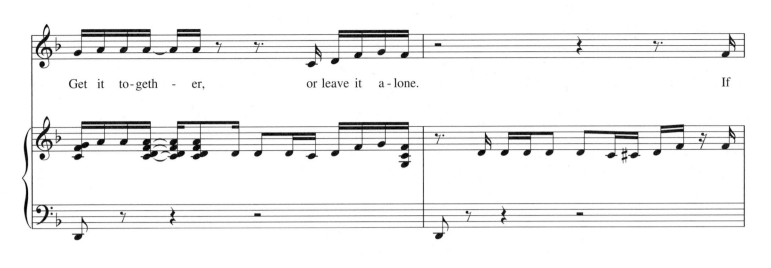

Get it to-geth - er, or leave it a-lone. If

you don't want my lov-in', I'll be gone. If

Get it to - geth - er, or leave it a - lone.

If you don't want_ my lov - in', I'll be gone.

Get up off your high horse, girl.

you don't want my lov-in', I'll be gone. (Gone, gone, gone, gone, gone.)

Think, girl, what you're do-in'.

Throw-in' this heart of mine all a-way. Oh,

think, girl, you know I love you. To

I WANT YOU BACK

Words and Music by FREDDIE PERREN,
ALPHONSO MIZELL, BERRY GORDY and DEKE RICHARDS

I'LL BE THERE

Words and Music by BERRY GORDY, HAL DAVIS,
WILLIE HUTCH and BOB WEST

You and I   must make   a pact;
Let me fill your heart with joy   and laugh - ter.

we must bring   sal - va - tion back.
To - geth - er - ness,   well, it's all   I'm af - ter.

Where there is   love,   I'll __ be there. __
When - ev - er you need me,   I'll __ be there. __

THE LOVE YOU SAVE

Words and Music by BERRY GORDY, ALPHONSO MIZELL,
FREDDIE PERREN and DENNIS LUSSIER

LOOKIN' THROUGH THE WINDOWS

Words and Music by
CLIFTON DAVIS

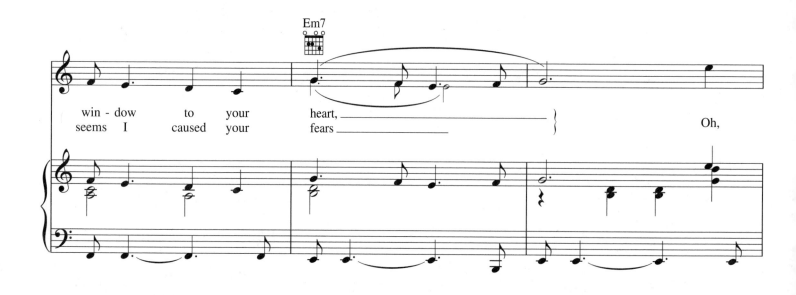

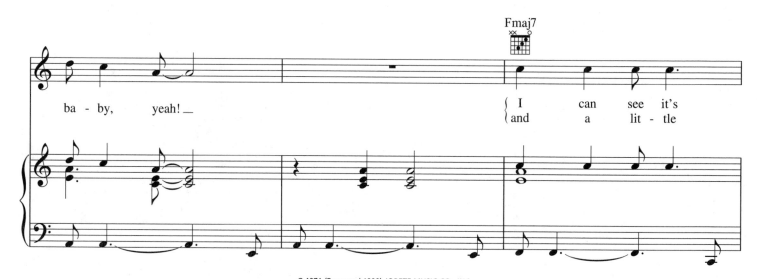

MAMA'S PEARL

Words and Music by FREDDIE PERREN, ALPHONSO MIZELL,
BERRY GORDY and DEKE RICHARDS

You send cold chills up and down my spine. _____

*Male vocal is sung at written octave.

NEVER CAN SAY GOODBYE

Words and Music by
CLIFTON DAVIS

MAYBE TOMORROW

Words and Music by BERRY GORDY, ALPHONSO J. MIZELL,
FREDERICK J. PERREN and DENNIS LUSSIER

SUGAR DADDY

Words and Music by ALPHONSO MIZELL, FREDDIE PERREN,
BERRY GORDY and DEKE RICHARDS

Male vocal sung at written octave.

fine, fine, blew__ your mind.__ Fi - n'ly thought I'd caught__ ya, and your
crown just fits me to a T.__ 'Cause you on - ly come a - round__ me just to

love was mine, all mine.__ I see you____ walk by with oth - er guys,__
pick up what you need.__ You just play____ on my e - mo - tions,__ with

To Coda ⊕

step, step, step-pin' on __ my toes. The whole town's talk-in' a-bout__ how I'm__ your
"Please, please, pret - ty, please?" Well, ev - 'ry-bod-y's got the no - tion I'm__ your

D.S. al Coda